What Color is *Your* Privilege?

What Color is *Your* Privilege?

F.I. Goldhaber

Opening a Window on the Suffering
Many are Privileged to Ignore

WHAT COLOR IS *YOUR* PRIVILEGE?
Opening a window on the suffering many are privileged to ignore

Copyright © 2022 by F. I. Goldhaber

All rights reserved. No part of this book may
be reproduced by any means without permission.

Cover images from depositphotos.com

ISBN 978-1-945824-56-2

First Left Fork Edition • September 2022

PO Box 110
O'Brien, OR 97534
www.leftforkbooks.com

Dedication

To the anarchists, abolitionists, activists, anti-fascists, aid groups, agitators, advocates, analyzers, and annalists of the Portland area.

You inspire me daily.

Content Warning

These poems disclose, describe, and denounce white supremacy, racism, terrorism, misogyny, rape, police brutality, Queer/Trans hatred, ableism, etc.

Table of Contents

Poetry	3
Hiding Words Won't Hide Damage	5
Respecting Beliefs	6
The Hypocrite's Creed	7
Hate	9
Shared Grieving	10
Little Old *White* Lady	11
Urban Warfare	13
The War on Terrorism	15
Home Grown Terrorism	17
Portland Heroes	18
#PortlandMassShooter	20
Grief	22
Summer in Three Cities	23
True Colors and False Flags	28
What Racism?	30
Thin Blue Lie	32
ACAB	33
Protest	34
Take The Knee	35
Lessons from Martin Niemöller	37
America the Beautiful	38
Envision	40
We Warned You	42
One Dress	45
Products for Sale	46
March 10, 2011	48
"Nice" People	51
Not Enough	52
Amendment XIV	55
Privileged	57

Contents, Cont'd

Where Have You Been?	59
Don't Touch My Hair	62
Hate Speech ≠ Free Speech	64
The Price of Prisons for Profit	66
Begging for Help	68
Times that Try	70
Normal Life	72
Blame Not the Virus	74
Trans Pacific Partnership	76
Disruptions	77
Eugenics	79
The Cost of Staying Alive	81
That Hurts	82
Forgive the Monster?	83
Getting Rid of the Gay	84
Words Matter	86
T	88
Gender Blending Fashion	89
Do I Pass?	90
Braving a Hostile World	92
#BiVisibility	94
#MeToo	95
Women's Lot	98
Who's Hurting?	100
She Only Screams at Night	102
Still Fighting	103
Not Our Fault	104
Explaining the Hashtags	105
Point of View	107
Intersectionality	108
On the Fringes	110

Growing up Jewish in the American South	111
Chains of Injustice	112
#NeverAgainIsNow	113
Protecting Hate	114
Persecution	115
Armed	117
Heartlands	118
Summer's Heat	119
Forgotten	120
Erased	122
Acknowledgments	125
About the Author	129

What Color is *Your* Privilege?

Poetry

I used to write poetry about
nature and food, love and cats, people
and places I observed. But, now, it
seems more and more I write poems to
berate what I see in this country.
So much hatred comes with so many
handles: racism, misogyny,
sectarianism, bigotry,
homomisiasm, nationalism.
How can I not excoriate the
horrific injustice, abuse, the
inequality, and corruption?

Now I write political, even
subversive, verse. Instead of flowers
my words describe voter suppression,
environmental destruction, the
proliferation of violence.
I orate about prisons filled with
people of color treated as slaves.
I rant about full-time workers who're
eligible for SNAP, Medicaid.
I slam attacks on LGBT
rights, decry government abuse, and
militarization of the police.

But, does anyone hear my words? Do
they heed my warnings? They sit and nod,
sometimes buy my books. Still they shop at
Wal-Mart, Amazon; claim bias no
longer exists; refuse to see how
corporate manipulation of
fear, anger, joy, laughter feed obscene
profits and billionaire wealth used to
purchase politicians, falsify
election results. I may waste breath,
but I'll speak until those silenced have
their voices restored, their rights returned.

Hiding Words Won't Hide Damage

The most *vulnerable*
among us suffer in
this mire of privileged
entitlement, where rich
white, straight, cis men refute
evidence-based data.
Where *diversity* is
denied, *transgender* folk
vilified, survival
of a *fetus* given
more value than the life
of the person who must
carry it to term. Where
science-based proof of climate
destruction is ignored
while doctrine based on myth
and deception becomes
the basis of our laws.

Respecting Beliefs

If your beliefs include marginalizing other people
because of their skin color, their religious faith, their gender,
their sexual orientation, their origin, their age;
If your beliefs allow justification for depriving
other people of their civil rights to life, liberty, and
happiness pursuits declared in seventeen seventy-six;
If your beliefs condone slaughter, rape, assault, subjugation,
imprisonment, execution of those you see as "others";
If your beliefs create stigmas to prevent those who appear,
think, love, or speak differently than you from making a living,
feeding their families, buying a home, earning retirement;
If your beliefs allow children to go to bed hungry, the
sick to go bankrupt, the disabled to struggle to survive,
the mentally ill to wander homeless, the store clerks to need
welfare benefits, the elderly to freeze through the winter;
If your beliefs prevent access to reproductive health care
while keeping young people ignorant about the facts of life
and the realities of sexual health, choices, and pleasure;
Then I'm under no obligation to respect your beliefs.
Keep your hate to yourself. Keep it out of our country, state, and
city laws, our schools, parks, stores, workplaces, and public restrooms.

The Hypocrite's Creed

All life is sacred and begins at conception, but we must
   deny life-saving medical care to the poor;
   deprive needy children of food, shelter, clothing;
   beat, bomb, shoot, hang to death men, women, children.

Deeply held religious beliefs require tax exemptions, and
   forbid paying for women's reproductive health;
   deny funds for science education/research;
   allow financing of civilian-killing drones.

Children are a gift from god, a reward from him, but we must
   rip children from their mother's breasts, their father's arms;
   warehouse them in tent cities despite extreme heat;
   cage, torment, and traumatize them while they're alone.

Religious freedom must always be protected, but we must
   ignore Muslims', Jews', Sikhs', Pagans', Hindus' rights;
   reject religions that conflict with our beliefs;
   obligate others to observe our holy days.

The bible is god's word, taken literally, but we must
   claim verses we disagree with are old fashioned;
   invent prohibitions never mentioned in text;
   judge harshly those who follow actual scripture.

States retain sovereignty and powers not assigned, but
   must not be allowed to legalize cannabis;
   can't protect the Internet from telecom greed;
   can't pass sanctuary laws to protect migrants.

We must save sex workers from human trafficking, but we must
   eliminate safe ways for them to find clients;
   force them onto the street, vulnerable to pimps;
   allow police to rape, rob, arrest, murder them.

The homeless crisis is a city emergency, but we must
   criminalize public camping, sitting, sleeping;
   protest attempts to open neighborhood shelters;
   fight rent control and minimum-wage increases.

Congress must cut taxes and frivolous spending, but must
   slash payments only for the rich, adding trillions to the debt;
   spend more on defense than seven countries combined;
   take food away from babies, seniors to compensate.

The hoax pandemic is now an emergency that requires
   huge corporate bailouts, no strings attached;
   loans to small businesses, with myriad conditions;
   pittance pay outs that won't cover rent to minimum-wage slaves.

All life is sacred and begins at conception, but we must
   only make testing available to the rich and celebrated;
   sacrifice seniors and children to save the stock market;
   prevent "prioritizing human life over economic stability."

Hate

Billy said we didn't start the fire.
But the world burns.
Muslims slaughter Christians in Iraq.
Yazidi flee.
Israelis and Gaza break truce once more.
Daesh fights Kurds.
Indians gang rape women daily.
Exiles swarm Chad.
Russia marches on Ukraine again.
Pakistan riots.
Azerbaijans kill Armenians.
Al-Qaeda plots.
Boko Haram kidnaps young girls, boys.
Syria bleeds.

And in the land of the free cops kill.
Unarmed Black men
executed by police daily.
Four Black deaths in
one month capture the nation's concern.
But we don't learn
of so many more who die only
because their skin
color offended men of privilege.
Driving while Black
in U.S., a capital offense.
Mothers teach sons
to raise hands, acquiesce ... but still
must bury them.

Shared Grieving

Every day people of color die.
Bombs in Yemen, shootings in Lebanon,
suicide explosions in Syria.
No one shouts out on Twitter, changes their
photo on Facebook, creates a hashtag.

But when terrorists kill white people in
European countries, you rally round
their flag, change your profile picture, add
a ribbon to show how you much care. But,
only if the victims look/believe like you.

Little Old *White* Lady

I saw you limp into the cellphone store and
beg for help with a phone disconnected by
a rival's service.

Behind the counter teenagers rattled off
terms you obviously didn't understand.
I called you over.

I explained in words of simpler times — before
the clerks were born. But, despite a balance, your
phone had been turned off.

T-Mobile demanded more money, which you
did not have, to turn it back on and wouldn't
refund your credit.

When you complained, they called the mall cops to throw
you out. Your story angered me, so I marched
down the street with you.

On the way to another T-Mobile store,
I learned you were a disabled Navy vet.
You told me stories.

When we arrived, I informed the clerk, "This man
needs his phone turned back on and I am here to
make sure you do that."

He looked in his computer. You showed him your
receipt. You stepped out to use my husband's phone
to ask for a ride.

He made a phone call and negotiated
with the person on line. You came back in to
hear your phone ringing.

I thanked the young man for his efforts. Thrilled, you
asked how I'd accomplished this miracle. I
whispered in your ear.

"Little old white lady," I said, much to your
amusement. For I can pass for white and took
advantage of that.

The clerks didn't see a man disabled in
service to the country they take for granted,
only dark brown skin.

They summoned cops when you insisted that they
rectify their employer's abuse and they
refused to help you.

As I left, I heard you gleefully shouting,
"Little old white lady." I'm glad I could help.
But, I'm not amused.

Urban Warfare

We arm police with military
surplus: flak jackets, gas masks, flash bangs,
riot shields, bayonets, machine guns,
APCs, helicopters, and tanks.
We created urban armies to
fight the misguided war on drugs which
devolved to hostilities against
citizens. Paramilitary
urban pacification forces
drill, waiting for opportunities
to attack, use their training, weapons.

The hammer sees every problem as
a nail. Soldiers see every person
who looks different as an enemy
combatant. Most officers are white.
People they routinely kill, tase, gas
have darker skin, kinky hair, accents.
White men traipse around stores brandishing
semi-automatic weapons while
unarmed Black teens and mentally ill
boys holding knives lie bleeding to death
in streets, guilty only of black skin.

Tactics, terror, and trampling rights in
the best traditions of Stasi and
Cheka make folks fear calling for help.
Nine-year-olds handcuffed, taken to jail
for playground fights. Rape victims, treated
as criminals, assaulted again.
Kids suffering mental health crises
killed in front of parents. Mothers and
fathers who have committed no crime tased
to the ground while their children wail.
Trans women jailed for carrying condoms.

Protestors sprayed with tear gas, mace while
peacefully assembling. Homeowners
woken by cops breaking down their doors,
grenades exploding in their baby's
crib, because someone did not write an
alleged dealers' address correctly.
We fill private prisons with people
of color, enslaving them at a
buck an hour, robbing them and their
children of any hope of breaking
free of poverty's endless cycle.

Claiming title to "America's
Finest," police insist they're proud to
protect and serve. But, who exactly?
They rally 'round themselves, fighting off
any charges of violating
civil liberties, overstepping
authority. They lie to shield each
other, challenge every dismissal
in court. They thwart any effort to
restrain them, turning off cameras
designed to protect the public.

Cops routinely torture innocents
to procure confessions. They ignore
evidence to obtain convictions.
How many years have those not guilty
served in prisons and sat on death row?
How many lives have courts stolen with
execution sentences based on
falsified evidence? If we do
not dismantle the military
machine patrolling our cities, the
blood shed tomorrow could well be yours.

The War on Terrorism

In the dictionary terrorists are
those who advocate terrorism, who
terrorize and frighten other people.

But, the media define terrorists
by the color of their skin. If you're white
you can shoot cops, slaughter Christians, blow up
buildings, form militias, slash throats, all
without being labeled a terrorist.

If you're arrested, you're taken into
custody, protected, allowed lawyers,
given a fair trial. You're a "lone gunman."

But walking down the street with black/brown skin,
swimming, selling cigarettes, carrying
toy guns, wearing costumes, buying candy,
soda, cigars, you are terrifying.

You're a thug, a hoodlum, a terrorist.
You frighten even the police. Those cops
become judge, jury, executioner.

You threaten them so they must grab you in
a choke hold, tase you, shoot you in the back.
You terrify them even if you're just
a girl, so they sit on you, pull your hair.

Right-wing white terrorists kill more in the
U.S. than Muslim zealots. But, who do
we ban; give up our freedoms in fear of?

Who do we send troops overseas to fight
and to slaughter? Our soldiers return home
in coffins or come back mutilated,
suffering from PTSD as well
as crippling physical injuries.

But when they step up to defend freedoms
they fought for — religion, speech, voting — it's
white homegrown terrorists who murder them.

Home Grown Terrorism

The hypocrites rage on, refusing to accept responsibility
when one of their own slaughters police, doctors, and innocent bystanders.
The rhetoric that sends terrorists to attack women seeking health care
erupts anew as those fomenting hate spew vitriol across airwaves.

No one questions why medical facilities find it necessary
to have safe rooms and armored doors. Too many accept how easily those
with criminal records and mental instability acquire weapons.

Those who immediately condemned all Muslims after some radical
fundamentalists violated their own religious texts to bomb and
shoot Parisians, urge us to wait for all the facts when their protégés
splatter the blood of strangers and destroy buildings on American soil.

Violent extremists threaten the U.S., but they call themselves "Christians,"
use Bibles not Qur'ans to justify destruction and murder. We won't
eradicate terrorism if we ignore the ones we raise at home.

Portland Heroes

"Shocking, un-Portland-like," a friend says.
But the tragedy is a perfect
portrait of Portland where skinheads killed
an Ethiopian student in
1988; where next door in
2000 an all-white jury
found a Black man was partially
responsible for being attacked
by skinheads; where police routinely
kill Black folk; where just last year a white
supremacist ran down and killed a
young Black man with his vehicle right
outside the city. But in Portland
not one, not two, but three men risked their
lives to help two teens harassed by a
fascist for being Black, for wearing
a hijab. Two died heroes, one a
veteran who survived Iraq and
Afghanistan only to lose his life
to a terrorist at home. But they
did not bleed out alone. Because in
Portland people stopped to help, saving
the life of a third. And three men chased
the murderer, helped police capture
him, ignored the bloody knife he thrust
at them, determined he would not harm
anyone else. Oregon is a

racist state, founded with prohibitions
against Blacks living here enshrined in
the constitution. It's home to gangs
of skinheads, white supremacists, and
fascists. But Portland is also a
place where people care, where they took to
the streets to protest the killings and
honor the heroes, where sometimes you
see more white faces than black at Black
Lives Matter marches because so few
Blacks live in this city and this state.

#PortlandMassShooter

A fan of the white teen who crossed state lines
to murder Black Lives Matter protesters
demonstrating against another white
police shooting of an unarmed Black man.
Groupie of an Asian fake journalist
who spews far-right propaganda non-stop
while constantly inciting violence
against anti-fascists, demonizing
them as armed extremists. The murderer
ranted on social media about
slaughtering protesters, houseless folk. He
exploded Saturday night, slaying a
disabled Senior, paralyzing a
second woman, and sending two others
to the hospital where they were treated
by the same doctors and nurses who saved
the life of the man who murdered their friend.

Police, the mayor, three commissioners,
press, fake journalists, reactionary
mouthpieces, all worked to build narratives
around righteous homeowner defending
himself, his property, from dangerous
armed thugs. They used "confrontation" and "clash,"
claiming no ties to extremism, no
political motives, while conflating
his savage, unprovoked, deadly attack
with other violence in the city.

But he doesn't own a home; advocates
killing peaceful protestors; is known as
a white supremacist sycophant of
Nazis, Proud Boys, right-wing terrorists; has
a record of abusing women and
threatening an unhoused man with a gun.

A master machinist who builds "ghost" guns
for those avoiding legal scrutiny.
Those he encountered warned police about
his death-dealing intentions for decades.

The unarmed women were in the street to
direct traffic, protect peaceful marchers
exercising their First Amendment right
to denounce police brutality. The
woman he murdered, a beloved corker,
collected food and clothing for those in
need, cooked and delivered hot dinners to
unhoused folk, brought people together, worked
to build community, improve the world.

Long after fascists filled their airwaves to
celebrate the blood shed, lionize the
butcher, and leftists revealed his name and
affiliations, his history of
domestic terrorism, his ties to
nationalists, ostracization from
various groups, violent incidents
of speech and action, police continued
obfuscating the truth, and denying
the reality, victim blaming and
gaslighting while lying about stealing
evidence from medics and protesters,
assigning an "investigator" known
for never arresting the person who
killed another activist years ago,
deceiving the public to protect a
killer many now believe has links to
white supremacists in the PPB.

Grief
(a Nonet)

So very many names. I try to
remember, but it's hard not to
miss a few. Cops keep adding
more. Is tonight's vigil
for their new victim
or tribute to
someone's year(s)
ago
death?

Summer in Three Cities

Invading Portland from other states and
distant towns, men came armed with hatred, fists,
baseball bats, brass knuckles, firearms, and more.

Police showed up in riot gear: Homeland
Security, Portland PD lined up
in front of white supremacists gathered
in the plaza.

But cops put their backs to the Nazis and
instead faced citizens who came to stand
against hate, to support inclusion and
diversity.

Cops fired rubber bullets at peacemakers,
threw flash bangs, thrust batons, deployed pepper
spray, arrested only those uniting
to face fascists.

Officers acted as judge, jury, and
executioner while lying about
justification for attacking a
peaceful protest.

Police protected those who brought hateful
rhetoric to their city, exchanging
greetings and playing football with the white
supremacists.

None of them were arrested even when
they stormed into other parks to incite
violence and "help" police arrest the
demonstrators.

Thousands were harmed by police action, their
eyes stinging, ears ringing, bruises from cops'
batons aching for days because they stood
up against hate.

Oblivious to the irony, cops
who are government employees guarded
those who advocate destroying the state
with blood and fire.

The fascists claim they rallied for free speech,
but that's just their code for the right to spew
vitriol at people of color, Jews,
Muslims, and Queers.

They have no interest in others' free
speech or anyone else's right to life,
liberty, or pursuit of happiness —
only their own.

They want civil liberties for themselves,
but no one else; religious freedom just
for those who believe the way they do; free
speech for *their* views.

And cops support this one-sided notion,
according fascists respect they deny
to women, POC, First Citizens,
LGBT.

Three thousand miles away in Charlottesville, police allowed out-of-state Nazis to attack locals who came to protest white supremacy.

A request for police protection for Jews attending Sabbath services was ignored, even though Nazis with rifles swaggered out front.

Police stayed out of the way and watched while Nazis beat, bloodied, and pointed guns at anyone who dared muster and speak out against fascists.

Even when white supremacists scuffled with police, none of them were arrested. Just some tickets for minor infractions were handed out.

Only the murderer was jailed and at first cops tried to claim that he must have feared for his life when he raced his car up and down crowded streets;

when he plowed his vehicle into throngs of counter-protestors, killing one young woman, seriously injuring at least nineteen more.

If he had been a dark-skinned Muslim, the cops would have instantly labeled him a terrorist. But he's white, pedestrians terrified him.

SWAT showed up in armored vehicles, aimed tear-gas grenade launchers at street medics treating victims before arrival of ambulances.

In St. Louis, cops randomly shot "non-
lethal rounds" at those who opposed yet one
more acquittal of a white cop who had
murdered Black men.

They behaved like Nazis, driving a car
through crowds of activists. Cops shouted "whose
streets, our streets" — taunting dissidents with Proud
Boys' rally cry.

A cop with his foot on a reporter's
neck sprayed pepper in his face. LEO
recklessly used chemical irritants
to attack folks.

Police kettled journalists with badges,
uniformed legal observers, medics,
righteously angry peaceful protestors,
those passing by.

Eager to jail hundreds, they locked up on
spurious charges news correspondents,
bystanders, and old women who could not
move fast enough.

Armed with military-grade weapons, in city after city the cops are the ones who break the laws and ignore the Constitution.

The president urges police to rough up suspects. The DOJ cuts back on federal oversight, refusing to stop racist cops.

We are marching into the abyss of history. How long before cops start goose stepping through the streets?

True Colors and False Flags

Millions of Black men imprisoned.
Thousands murdered by the police.
Entire neighborhoods under siege.

Black life in America means
underemployment, poverty,
endless unwarranted traffic
stops, other acts of harassment.

The Black Lives Matter rallies have
attracted white supporters both
online and in real life. Millions
denounce the abuse, rail against
militarized police forces.

But, when Blacks started shooting back,
even progressive advocates
could have second thoughts, finding
it easier to stay away,
keep quiet, and lament only
the loss of law enforcement lives.

What if someone is recruiting
the shooters? Ex-military,
radicalized, suffering from
Post Traumatic Stress Disorder
and racial profiling. Easy
targets for anyone who wants
to instigate a race war.

A war to justify further
escalation of violent
responses to peaceful protests;
rationalize expansion of
online government surveillance;
validate increasing budgets.

Innocuous statements freely
misconstrued, resulting in jail
for guiltless civilians.
Innocent people will bleed; too
many more will needlessly die.

So simple to maintain power
by turning citizens against
each other, using differences
to keep everyone divided.

Millions of Black men imprisoned.
Thousands murdered by the police.
Entire neighborhoods under siege.

What Racism?

We give our police officers
permission to kill citizens
of color with impunity.
Time after time, state officials
stage grand jury hearings that do
not return indictments against
cops who killed unarmed Black men who
annoyed them. No trial, no penalty.
Media ignore cops' records,
histories of abuse, firings, race
hatred, and profiling. But the step-
relatives of Black victims are
vilified for unrelated
transgressions. How many times do
white Americans try to claim
that racism in this country
is so yesterday? But they don't
have to bury their children. Cops
do not even question them for
actions that get Black men gunned down,
beaten, choked, and tasered to death.
The confederate flag, symbol
of slavery, oppression, hate,
and racism still flies over
southern capitol domes, still taunts
every Black man, woman, child.
Every day, cops kill people
of color — many innocent,
most unarmed. Still whites refuse to
see the systemic racism.

Ignoring that truth allows them
to be shocked when white nationalists
combine the college created
by slave owners with laws designed
to disenfranchise people of
color to steal our country and
send it hurtling back into times
even more hostile than today.

Thin Blue Lie

Not peace officers.
Bullies in uniform.
Demand that protesters stop
impeding vehicle traffic,
then block the same streets just vacated.
Close the sidewalks so demonstrators have
nowhere to go. Always making excuses
to attack with weapons of war: tanks, grenades, smoke
bombs, batons, sonic cannons, chemicals, poison gas.
No regard for law, civil rights, any consequences.
Injuring and arresting journalists, lawyers, civilians.
Blatantly lying the next morning, claiming dissidents engaged
in criminal acts of violence, throwing projectiles at police.
When in truth, the only assaults, shootings, riots, and other carnage were
committed by police who put lives, safety, and the First Amendment
      at risk.

ACAB
(a Shadorma)

Black, white, brown.
Skin color gets lost
behind the
uniform,
badge, and weapon enforcing
white supremacy.

Protest

Reverend George registered to vote.
Linda just wanted to walk to school.
Medgar applied to attend law school.
Rosa took a seat and would not budge.
Ezell, Franklin, Joseph, and David
insisted on the right to buy lunch.
Martin spoke about a dream he had.
John's dedication spans five decades.
Colin knelt during national anthems.

All these African American
men, women, and children angered whites
who refused to respect them and to
accept their equality; denied
them their dignity and civil rights.
Some paid with their lives, some only jail.
All suffered scorn and rebuke because
they refused to accept injustice;
spoke against systemic racism.

Take The Knee

Red, white, and blue,
a piece of cloth
that represents
subjugation
of Black people,
massacre of
Indigenous
nations, abuse
of Latinos,
exploitation
of Asian folk,
persecution
of non-christians,
murder of
LGBT
and those who are
other gendered.

You want to sing
an anthem of
war before a
violent game
but take umbrage
when the athletes
who entertain
you take a knee
in memory,
to remind you that
their prowess and
affluence don't
protect them from
cops who slaughter
Black men who dare
to drive, to breathe,
to speak their minds.

You claim to be
a patriot
but deny them rights
enshrined in the
Constitution
you pretend to
honor, revere,
and adhere to,
including rights
to peaceably
assemble and
petition for
a redress of
their grievances,
to speak against
inequality
and injustice.

But you ignore
the amendments
that accord non-
whites the same rights
and privileges
you consider
sacrosanct, and
blame the victims
of systemic
racism when
they take a knee
to remind the
world that they
risk their lives
just because their
skin has darker
tones than yours.

Lessons from Martin Niemöller

Epigraph:
"First they came for the Socialists, and I did not speak out—because I was not a Socialist."

Thousands of unarmed, dark-skinned men shot by police.
You've done nothing, your skin is white.

Hundreds of mentally ill of all colors killed.
You've done nothing, your mind is clear.

Dozens of Black trans women slayed year after year.
You did nothing, you're cis and white.

Police murdered a white woman who called for help.
You did nothing, she's Australian.

We demanded police wear body cameras
and paid millions to purchase them.

But those cameras always seem to "malfunction"
When the truth is inconvenient.

Officer Friendly has disappeared, replaced by
urban soldiers equipped for war.

When all those in uniform are hammers,
the rest of us look just like nails.

You ignored the lessons of history, voted
for a madman's fascist regime.

You chose white supremacy rather than accept
cultural change, social progress.

You've remained silent or excused the attacks. What
will you do when they come for you?

America the Beautiful

"America is better than this"
Only if you're white, straight, cis, neurotypical.
For the rest of us, America is
   the land of genocide, slavery, concentration camps;
     of pogroms and police violence;
        of doors battered down, blood on the streets,
           mass graves discovered a century after the smoke clears.

"America is the land of the free, home of the brave"
Only if you're white, male, xtian, English speaking.
For the rest of us, America is
   the land of persecution and prisons populated
     with people whose only crime is dark skin,
        accents, queerness, neurodivergence, gender nonconformity,
          not worshiping the evangelical prosperity gospel.

"America first"
Only in military spending, medical debt, poverty, incarcerations, gun deaths.
For the rest of us, America is last
   among "first world" countries in
     infant and maternal mortality, food security,
        access to health care, longevity, income equality,
          literacy, parental leave, vacations, mental health.

"We must protect our democracy"
For white property owners, America was a Republic.
For the rest of us, the Constitution never uses that word and
   the structure of these United States discourage Democracy with
     an Electoral College preventing democratic election of a president,
        a Second Amendment preserving slave patrol militias, and a
          Three Fifths compromise giving slave states more power.

America where "it can't happen here"
Only if you close your eyes to the patterns.
For the rest of us, we see "others" labeled as criminals, perverts, threats.
   Populist politicians, government propaganda, travel bans;
      children shivering in filthy, over-crowded cages;
         police slaughtering POC, LGBTQ, the mentally ill;
      homeless people disappearing; cultural genocide.

We know what's coming. Do you?

Envision

Envision removing cops.
It's easy if you try.
No more unarmed Black
men slaughtered in the streets.
Imagine all the fam'lies
peacefully prospering.

No more rigged out bullies
putting Black girls in cuffs
or shooting young Black boys.
It's not that far a stretch
to envision intact,
flourishing neighborhoods.

Envision no prisons.
It's not that hard to do.
No cages to lock folks
up in nor slave labor.
Imagine all people
Living without fear, dread.

You may call me fantast.
But I'm not alone at
all. I wish you could see
how much better a world
we could build without an
oppressive police force.

Envision aborting
capitalism, I
wonder if you can. No
more homeless, hungry
Queer folk living on streets.
No more exploitation.

Envision health care and
education, housing,
and healthy food for all.
Eliminating rich
men's wars for fossil fuels
so we all live in peace.

We Warned You

Seriously? You're "surprised"? "Speechless"?
You insist we do something *right* now?
WTF have *you* been? Blissfully
posting brunch selfies on Instagram?

"Who thought we'd ever come to this??" Just
all of us who are poor, disabled,
Queer, Trans, neurodivergent; who have
darker skin, accents, different beliefs.

We all begged you to pay attention.
We warned you of nefarious plans.
They've marched on this warpath for almost
half a century, yet you're at a loss?

You ignored history, politics,
blatant lies, and Nazi takeovers.
You vilified those alerting you
to the approaching apocalypse.

You kept saying, "Vote blue no matter
who." Even for someone who broke all
his campaign pledges? Who enabled
the prison pipeline in '94?

Who wrote the law allowing cops to
steal your property without trial or
filing charges? Who made relief from
student loan abuse more difficult?

Who claimed the 1973
decision went too far because he
didn't think women have the sole right
to say what happens to their bodies?

The decision leaked while the Speaker
of the House, majority leader,
and whip stumped in Texas on behalf
of an anti-choice blue incumbent.

Vote blue to protect choice, you extolled.
And yet, that right's vanished for those poor.
The right to marry, even make love,
for same sex partners disappears next.

What exactly have *you* done the last
few decades while they ground hard won rights
of Black, Trans, Queer, et al folk to dust?
Pointless protests in pink pussy hats?

But you won't strike against employers
or boycott corporate enablers,
'cause that might require forgoing some
of your own comfort and convenience.

More people have died of Covid since
the last election. More children starved.
More immigrants imprisoned. More folks
forced to live in tents, harassed by cops.

Folks lined up for hours to vote blue — in
unbearable cold, oppressive heat.
All for naught. Just virtue signaling
and performative finger wagging.

Blue had so many options: reign in
misbehaving members, utilize
executive orders, expand the
court. Red shows them ways to get things done.

But, blue grift just chases fund-raising
windfalls with more empty assurances.
Because only red keeps promises.
Blue just makes excuses why it can't

while red burns books, bans education
not aligned with white supremacy,
disenfranchises blue voters, and
willfully creates dire poverty.

One Dress
(a Nonet)

For the price of that one dress you could
feed a family, pay their rent.
The cost of shoes alone would
cover medical care,
prescriptions. Spending
on hair, makeup
would reduce
other
bills.

Products for Sale

If the service is free,
you're not the customers,
your data's the product.

They're building an online
portrait of your preferred
colors, drinks, pets, books, films.

Lest you further enrich
tech multimillionaires,
refuse to share most things.

Do not play games; sign up
for no events; ignore
all the click bait and ads.

Companies entice you
to hand valuable
information to them
for the privilege of
seeing kitten pictures
or playing Candy Crush.

Cling to what's left of your
privacy, post only
what you're willing to let
your mom, the IRS,
religious relatives,
your worst enemies see.

Facebook, Google, LinkedIn,
Pinterest, Instagram,
Tumblr, Reddit, and more
sell your data to those
trying to convince you
to purchase junk you don't
need, food you shouldn't eat.

No longer consumers,
you are being consumed
while their bank balances,
stock portfolios, and
political clout thrive.

March 10, 2011

Epigraph:
"Then they came for the trade unionists, and I didn't speak out—because I wasn't a trade unionist."
—*Pastor Martin Niemöller*

Last night the end started.
The only question: end of what?

For decades, the rich abused
the middle class, trying to take
us back to times of serfs,
peasants, and slaves. Union blood

bought us forty-hour work
weeks, two days off, pensions, health care
benefits. The middle
class expanded to include more

than merchants, small business
owners. The rich rebelled, taking
their jobs and paychecks to
China, India. The

U.S. prospers, but all
the money goes into only
a few pockets. They trashed
our economy, destroyed the

value of our homes, the
only asset most of us own,
and stole the taxes that
should have repaired roads, taught children,

protected our safety,
delivered quality health care
to us all. They monger
fear, set religious believers

against each other. Last
night they dropped all pretense of a
budget crisis, broke the
law, came for the trade unionists.

Last night the end started.
The only question: end of what?

Will the American
people finally wake up to
the outrageous, horrid,
parasitic travesties the
GOP perpetuated

on us all? Will they stop
allowing the GOP to
ignore/remove/destroy
our Constitutional rights? Or

did we hear the death knoll
of the Democratic party,
last night? Cash from corporate
America and the 400

who own more than millions
inundates the GOP with
ample funds to buy votes
in Congress for more tax breaks and

opportunities to
abuse what's left of the middle
class. Only the unions
have enough money to
fight back. Only the unions stand

between us and return
to a world run by dictators
and robber barons. The
ultra right-wing resorted to

lies and fabrications
against organizations that
register and recruit
minority, poor, and liberal

voters. Only unions
can compete against them. So the
big-money backers of
the Republican governor

have manufactured a
crisis to take out the unions
in Wisconsin, using
public policy to destroy

their only rival. Should
their union busting succeed in
Wisconsin, Ohio,
Indiana, Pennsylvania,

they will come for the rest.
All the big political cash
to decide who wins and
loses elections will support

right-wing candidates. Bake
sales versus billionaires, what the
future of elections
will look like if we don't speak up.

Last night the end started.
The only question: end of what?

"Nice" People

Germans who collaborated,
who turned away from the horror,
may have been thought ordinary
citizens. But they were not "nice."

There are no "well-meaning" racists,
"kind" white supremacists, "sweetheart"
homomisiasts, or "good guy"
misogynists. They are not "nice."

Those who choose to look the other
way, to ignore politics, and
to focus on happier things
are not "nice." They are complicit.

They may want to believe they are
"nice." If you are related, you
may want to believe they are "nice."
But, oppression is never "nice."

They may be ignorant, they may
claim lack of privilege because
they are poor, uneducated,
disabled. But, they are not "nice."

The time has come to choose. Fascist
or Antifa. Capitalist
or socialist. Colonizer
or resistance. In every
case, only the latter is "nice."

Not Enough

Your tears are not enough.
Your prayers are not enough.
Your shares are not enough.
Your hashtags are not enough.

Your grief for one dead Black man
will not erase systemic
racism that has imbued
this country since its founding.

Get off Facebook. Take to the
streets. If only black faces
show up, protesters will be
dismissed as rabble rousers.

Bear witness. Take videos
and distribute them to lift
the veil of secrecy from
rampant police malfeasance.

Your tears are not enough.
Your prayers are not enough.
Your shares are not enough.
Your hashtags are not enough.

Demand police accept blame,
face murder charges, prison.
Punish cops who refuse to
testify against their own.

Insist on changing laws that
target POC, protect
cops. Fire judges who send Black
men to prison but not white.

Recognize your privilege.
Use it to foster change, to
hold others accountable.
Don't shrug off racist jokes, posts.

Your tears are not enough.
Your prayers are not enough.
Your shares are not enough.
Your hashtags are not enough.

Leave the echo chamber and
expand your world view. Read books
written by POC, buy
POC movies, music.

Teach your children to respect
diversity. Expose them
to stories featuring non-
white heroes and good guys.

Educate your parents, your
Fox News watching uncle, and
your neighbor who displays the
confederate flag inside.

Your tears are not enough.
Your prayers are not enough.
Your shares are not enough.
Your hashtags are not enough.

Don't accept the status quo.
Never assume it's only
someone else's affliction.
Police murder white men, too.

Don't condone cop shootings, but
don't blame all POC for
their deaths. Accept that we all
suffer when race wars explode.

Racism creates toxic
environments that only
hate can sustain. That poison
is tearing our world apart.

Your tears are not enough.
Your prayers are not enough.
Your shares are not enough.
Your hashtags are not enough.

Amendment XIV

Epigraph:
"All persons born or naturalized in the United States, and subject to the jurisdiction thereof, are citizens of the United States and of the state wherein they reside."

To start they come for the "anchor
babies," stripping citizenship
from the first generations born
on U.S. soil.

Then they come for the grandchildren
of immigrants, those with parents
born here, imprisoning them in
concentration.

Creating laws based on gender,
skin color, sexuality,
religion. Depriving us of
life and liberty.

Stealing property without due
process of law, denying us
protection equal to white, straight,
cis, christianists.

They claim to revere the U.S.
Constitution, but as from their
bible, only those passages
that justify

vilifying those they hate and
benefitting those they see as
"true" Americans, ignoring
their own status

as children of immigrants and
invaders, their history of
enslaving and slaughtering the
First Peoples here.

No one will be left to speak up
for them when all their corporate
masters finally lock the shackles
around their necks.

Privileged

You labored hard to get where you are
    struggled,
    studied,
    networked,
    did the work,
    you earned it.

You ignore others who labored just as hard
    struggled,
    studied,
    networked,
    did the work,
    got nowhere.

Because of their skin color, gender
    sexuality,
    disabilities,
    neurodivergence,
    religion,
    poverty.

Because systemic racism, misogyny,
    heteronormativity,
    neurotypicality, and racism
    deprived them of
    the same opportunities
    you took for granted.

Because authoritarian governments
    deny them education,
    jobs, housing,
    civil rights,
    health care,
    equality.

Not all those who
    struggled,
    studied,
    networked,
    did the work,
    reaped the rewards.

If you never had
    to wait for a court
    to decide if you've
    the same rights (or not)
    as everyone else,
    you have privilege.

Where Have You Been?

Millions of white women took to the streets
wearing pink pussy hats, carrying signs,
proudly posting their clever slogans on
Facebook, Twitter, YouTube, and Instagram.

The police waved as they went by. No one
arrested; no riot gear in sight; not
a whiff of tear gas or pepper spray; no
flash bangs, rubber bullets, kettling.

Women gathered by hundreds of thousands
in cities around the world, on seven
continents, to protest installation
of white supremacists in Washington.

But Women of Color, Indigenous,
Queer, Trans, and immigrant activists could
only ask, "Where've you been all these years while
they beat, shot, arrested, deported us?"

"Where were you while white patriarchy stole
our lives, lands, freedoms, civil rights; murdered
Trans women, assaulted Queers, raped Native
women, shipped Latinas far from their homes?"

More than half of the white women in the
U.S. voted to put xenophobic,
racist, homo hating, misogynists
in the White House. But now they demonstrate?

Those who've been marching, resisting; getting
gassed; shot with "non-lethal" rounds and water
cannons; bleeding and dying; wasting time
in jail; watched in anger at the contrast.

They might allow newcomers to join their
resistance because the danger is so
much greater than white women perceive. The
battle weary don't have time to explain.

Allies are needed. Action's required. But
neophytes must be willing to do more
than march with punny signs and knitted caps.
They must respect and learn from the vanguard.

This fight isn't just about equal pay,
workplace harassment, reproductive health
care, school athletics. It's an ongoing
horrific, bloody, life and death struggle.

For people of other colors, genders,
physical abilities, religions,
sexuality; for immigrants and
refugees this isn't just a parade.

Police don't pose for selfies with them when
they take to the streets after another
unarmed Black man is slaughtered, their access
to clean water destroyed, their land stolen.

So many white women come late to the
challenge. They never had police pull their
hair, sit on them, bash in their heads. They've not
been harassed, orphaned, raped, widowed by cops.

White women ignored racism, hatred,
bigotry, slaughter. To move forward, they
must suppress their fragile white egos, step
up, do more, or they just wasted their time.

They must heed those who've
spent centuries fighting for life, freedom;
who've watched their loved ones bleed out in the streets;
suffered cold steel biting into their wrists.

Set pride aside, recognize privilege,
understand how much more other women
endure. Advancing straight white women's lives
won't help Queer or Trans women of color.

But restraining police, working to end
systemic racism, forcing Congress
to enshrine civil rights for all peoples,
will improve the welfare of everyone.

If this poem offends, if you question
its message, if the election results
surprised you, then open your eyes to the
suffering you're privileged to ignore.

Don't Touch My Hair

Throughout history hair
revealed religious faith,
social standing, power, wealth.

Many societies
regarded hair as a
woman's crowning glory.

Wealthy women wore styles
so elaborate they
required hours of effort.

Religions, demanding
modesty, insisted
women cover their hair.

The Qing dynasty forced
male subjects to wear the
Manchu queue or face death.

Louisiana laws
required free Black women
hide their hair with Tignons.

Punjab Police forced the
Sikh to cut their hair. Mobs
sheared Jewish men's peyot.

Sports organizations,
schools, workplaces compel
ethnic men and women

to change how they wear their
hair so they conform to
colonialist norms.

Genetics plays a role
in color, texture, curl,
thickness, potential length.

Curling irons, dyes, pins,
oils, relaxers, scissors,
combs, impose compliance

and allow privileged
appropriation, theft
of culture without the

consequences brought by
racism, bigotry,
and discrimination.

For the long lustrous locks
of Asians and Native
American peoples

and delicate helix
curls indigenous to
Africans are often

fetishized by those with
more advantages, who
have less "exotic" hair.

Without consent they touch.
They may profess envy,
praise their victims' beauty.

But in reality,
they flaunt entitlement
with rudeness and disdain.

Hate Speech ≠ Free Speech

Hate speech is not free speech when it drowns
out the voices of others; when it's
used to harass those with darker skin;
when it incites violence, murder.

I'd abandoned your institution
long ago because you were always
so eager to defend nazis' and
white supremacists' right to free speech.

Your organization ignores the
impact of white privilege on the
conversation; trauma inflicted
on POC targets of hatred.

But after the election, when you
jumped to fight for immigrants and geared
up to oppose the tyrant in the
White House, I forgave past transgressions.

My mistake. For only weeks after
I rejoined, you again defended
the indefensible — the "right" to
incite violence with hate speech.

Just nine days after one of their own
slaughtered two men and wounded a third
because they dared to stand between him
and the recipients of his hate,

you stood up to fortify fascist
falsehoods, sanctioning the lie that their
rally had anything to do with
"free speech" when it was all about hate.

Now, you have more blood on your hands, for
enabling a rally that turned deadly,
defending nazis' "rights" to hold a
city hostage, attack its people.

Will you send representatives to
funerals, compensate families?
Or will you ignore the hateful truth
until the Gestapo comes for you?

The Price of Prisons for Profit

You ignore millions of people of color incarcerated
for petty crimes — some innocent — imprisoned without hope, deprived
of contact with families, proper nutrition, medical aid.

You reject myriad mentally ill patients jailed without their
medications or psychiatric care, treated like animals
by sadistic guards who don't even allow them to know the time.

Left to psychologically rot in jail, often with no pillows
or blankets; bereft of in-person contact by monetary
setups that charge more than they can afford for video visits;

Denied access to life affirming hormones, always misgendered,
abused by both guards and fellow prisoners for daring to ask
for acceptance of identities outside binary genders;

Forced to work for pennies an hour manufacturing garments,
furniture, electronics, and more so corporations that pay
no taxes can claim their merchandise is made in America;

Caged for twenty-three hours a day, prevented from sleeping, hungry,
alone, required to pay hundreds to the governments trampling their
rights and destroying their health; these wretches escape your attention.

Until the trap of private, pecuniary, prisons captures
someone you love, subjecting them to the tortures others endure
day in and day out across the U.S. from sea to shining sea.

Only then do you complain about corruption, assail abuse,
deride the debasement, impugn inequities and injustice,
and discover organizations that have fought this for decades.

You retain attorneys, pay for visits, purchase comfort from the
commissary. You advocate for reform, write letters to your
legislators, and sign online petitions to the president.

But those who do not have families with resources perish in prison, expiring from exploitation, strangled by their sorrow, succumbing to suicide, murdered via medical neglect.

Once the ordeal ends for your own victim of prisons for profit, will you continue to campaign for those who have no such support? Or will you forget that your loved one's journey is hardly unique?

Will you return to ignoring the relationships ravaged, the communities crippled by losing those sucked into schemes designed to dehumanize any who're minorities, moneyless, mad?

Begging for Help

Why do you find it acceptable
living in a country where people
who get sick, injured, disabled must
beg for cash to pay medical bills?

Where not only pharmaceutical
makers, hospitals, and insurance
companies enrich their stockholders
on other people's misery, but

crowd-funding sites and credit cards make
a killing (sometimes literally)
off the suffering of struggling
victims of crime, other tragedies.

How does the richest country in the
world tolerate people compelled to
beg for charity when pushed over the edge
by circumstances beyond control?

This is the world austerity built —
health care only for the rich, others
forced to live one paycheck away from
bankruptcy and homelessness, sometimes
choosing between food and medicine.

Where bearing a child, being raped, or
just being born female is a pre-
existing condition allowing
insurers to deny coverage.

Republicans strive to destroy the
ability of labor unions
to protect workers from
exploitation, injury, and death,

eliminating OSHA, worker's
compensation, insurance, sick leave,
vacations, even weekends, children
working, and any minimum wage.

They would eradicate pensions and
Social Security, requiring
seniors to eat cat food or starve, if
influenza does not kill them first.

Restricting women's agency, the
GOP wants to deny access
to any reproductive care then
penalize mothers for giving birth.

They claim to be pro-life, but that ends
at delivery when those born poor,
with dark skin, Queer, Trans, suffering from
disabilities, whose parents don't

speak English or worship Jesus, are
denied housing, medical care, food,
education, jobs, life, liberty,
or hope of pursuing happiness.

Times that Try

These times try our souls in the court of adversity
as a global pandemic reveals our true natures.

Some reached out, helped where they could: providing free lunch
to students who only eat at school; running errands
for home-bound, frightened seniors; donating needed funds,
supplies, masks; offering amusements, delivery.

Buying gift cards and meals to donate and deliver
to health care workers, helping struggling restaurants
while thanking those risking their lives serving every day.

But scammers, hackers, bankers, politicians only
saw an opportunity for profit. Dumping stock;
gouging prices; forcing employees to risk their health;
sacrificing a thousand lives for a market bump.

Taking advice from Wall Street instead of doctors and
scientists; refusing to lock down and prevent the
viral spread; delaying tests in search of more profits;
denying sick leave, health care; bailing out megacorps.

Partying on the beach rather than forgo spring break
festivities; gathering at clubs and restaurants;
choosing to endanger the old and vulnerable,
unwilling to make sacrifices for common good.

Demanding at-risk employees return to work in
hospitals; abandoning the innocent in care
facilities; ignoring risks to immigrants in
concentration camps, POC in profit prisons.

Maliciously pushing harmful snake oil, defective
supplies; stealing tips from those who deliver; coughing
on bus drivers; licking groceries, parcels, door knobs.

Ammosexuals gathering on state capitol
steps — armed with automatic weapons, racism, white
supremacy — threatening those trying to protect
the lives of everyone except the imprisoned.

The trial of souls in the court of adversity and
so many fail to exhibit basic compassion.

Normal Life

You have a nice home to shelter in,
food to eat, shows to stream, games to play.

You don't live with an abuser or
parents who misgender you; insist
your orientation is sinful.

Yet you complain you're deprived of your
social life, restaurants, bars, park visits.

You don't need to risk your life and your
loved ones for minimum wage
without protection, sick leave, health care.

You've enough to pay your bills; credit
cards to order online; connected
devices allowing well-paid work.

But you miss the ball games, parties,
band performances, church services.

You don't shiver in the cold, snow, and
rain under a tent if you're lucky,
or just a cardboard box, or blanket.

If your throat is sore, your head feels hot,
you can telephone *your* physician.

You don't have to stand in line for a
clinic that sends you home when they run
out of test kits. Or just keep working.

You know what the virus looks like, how
to prevent exposure and illness.

You don't toil next to those who could be
infected with no information
how, or supplies to, protect yourself.

You fret about event and concert
cancellations, missed graduations.

You don't worry about untreated
broken bones; forced sex without access
to birth control; deadly pregnancy.

The only people desperate for
life to return to normal are those
privileged to enjoy "normal" life.

Blame Not the Virus

Covid19 isn't killing millions.
Scientists, virologists, epidemiologists
warned of its approach for decades.
Governments failed to take note. To prepare.
Blame those governments for the deaths of millions.

Covid19 doesn't steal medical supplies.
For-profit "health care" companies decimated supplies,
equipment, protective gear, because manufacturing
and storage cost money that can line CEO pockets.
Blame those CEOs for the dearth of medical supplies.

Covid19 doesn't target health care workers.
Hospital mega corps force underpaid aides,
nurses, doctors, to work without proper
staffing, masks, gloves, and other PPE.
Blame those mega corps for dead health care workers.

Covid19 doesn't prey on "essential" workers.
The one percent block minimum-wage raises, medical
insurance, and sick leave so they can look magnanimous
when they drop chump change into charity buckets.
Blame billionaires for dying grocery store workers, delivery drivers.

Covid19 hasn't destroyed the economy.
Capitalism and corporatocracy already did that,
leaving millions destitute with no access to health care,
sufficient income to survive; buried under mountains of debt.
Blame capitalism for the economy's destruction.

Covid19 takes no responsibility for legislation.
Congress decided to give billionaires blank checks
and begrudge minimum-wage slaves a month's rent,
adequate unemployment, eviction protection.
Blame Congress owned by those billionaires for pork belly legislation.

Covid19 makes no false claims about masks, cures, vaccines.
White Supremacists elected a racist idiot
who eschewed science and promoted anything
his grifter supporters and sycophants profit from.
Blame White Supremacists for dangerous snake oil, anti-vax deceit.

Covid19 didn't choose to linger, manifesting variant after variant.
Petri dishes of the unvaccinated
who refused to isolate became hosts
for more virulent and infectious mutations.
Blame anti-vaxxers for the never-ending pandemic.

Covid19 didn't take us to the brink of our own destruction.
Two centuries of spewing extracted fossil fuels into the air,
corporations abdicating responsibility
for extirpating the environment pushed us to the edge.
Blame billionaire tax shelters for humanity's extermination.

Trans Pacific Partnership

First Abraham Lincoln let them live longer than people.
Then the U.S. Supremes gave them personhood and freedom.
Privileges of citizenship — free speech and the pretense of religion
— to gain tax reductions and eliminate workers' rights.

The president wants to allow their interests to supersede
sovereign nations' ability to serve their people.
Laws protecting safety, clean air, public health, will be waived
if it's possible they'll inhibit corporate profits.

Protection of corporate revenue will usurp all
individual rights to free expression, privacy,
due process, and the ability to afford housing,
food, medical care, education, transit, internet.

Forget about human rights. Only corporate power
carries any weight. They bought the U.S. government and
many of the world's leaders, jailing any who speak out.
They negotiate in secret to take away more rights.

Disruptions

I must admit I laughed
when I read about the
cables cut by anchors.

All the companies that
sent their jobs overseas;
laid off employees here
by the tens of thousands;
who said they had to move
facilities offshore
to stay competitive.

Blurring our sense of self,
emphasizing our roles
as cogs in their machines.

They lost Internet and
telephone connections.

Under the ocean's surf,
disturbing the sea life,
fiber optic cables
bind the world together
with communication.

Someone's carelessness caused
the loss of contact with
their underpaid Chinese
and Indian workers.

Now new viruses run
rampant through factories,
halting production,
deterring shipping, ruining
executive travel
and recruitment planning.

Call centers and IT
services brought to a
halt by shelter in place.

Global economies
disrupted by a mere
microorganism.

Panic throwing markets
into disarray,
destroying delusions
of prosperity.

Who's in charge of this mess?
Because if we're betting
between a virus and
capitalism, my
money's on the former.

Eugenics

She said the quiet part out loud,
people "unwell to begin with"
don't deserve to live. Just like the
poor, the Black, the Indigenous,
the immigrants, the Queers, the Trans.

Because once they figured out most
victims were marginalized, had
comorbidities, were "others,"
the fight to eliminate the
virus succumbed to the battle
to save the economy god.
In the name of the Profit you
must sacrifice the grandparents,
disabled veterans, nannys'
children, baristas' mothers, clerks
at the corner stores, restaurant
servers, health care workers, drivers
bringing groceries, carry out.

The U.S. already makes clear
who is not wanted, including
those with disabilities, pre-
existing conditions, other
gods, languages, and cultural
traditions. No skin tones kissed with
melanin or "natural" hair.

Disposable collateral,
oblations necessary to
avoid missing brunch, a concert,
a chance to go out dancing or
cheer for the home team at a pub.
Millions already dead, millions
more permanently disabled to
ensure the privileged's comfort,
the corporations' bottom lines,
billionaires' stock portfolios.

As we tumble into Nazi
sovereignty it's worth reminding
those gambling with their own health and
risking the lives of others, that
among the first slaughtered in the
German Holocaust were those who're
disabled by the "Spanish" flu.

The Cost of Staying Alive

Ten times a day
I prick a finger,
squeeze out a drop of blood
and wait for the number that
will determine what I do next.

Must I pierce my
skin again, this time
using needles that screw
onto pens I then use to
inject units of insulin?

Or do I need
to eat, even if
I do not hunger and
have no interest in food
of any kind at the moment?

The meter rules
my life, decides what,
when, and whether I eat
while I fight for insurance
coverage to pay for the strips

required to make
it work, strips that cost
as much as a dollar
apiece, ten bucks a day, more
than three thousand greenbacks yearly.

When combined with
fifty cents for each
needle, sixty bucks for
two days' insulin supply,
that's a high price to stay alive.

That Hurts

You slapped me on the shoulder,
the one I dislocated
many years ago. That hurts.

You reach out to shake my hand.
I point to the hidden splint.
You grab for the other, but
I wear a brace to protect
it too. Even if you just
gently squeeze either of my
enervated hands, that hurts.

I must dodge and defend from
amiable aggression,
affectionate attacks, and
affable abuse that hurts.

Your cordial clap on my back
wakens persistent pain and
requires ice to recover,
costs me the ability
to attend an event or
write a new poem. You stole
one of my spoons and that hurts.

Why is it acceptable
to slam strangers, cuff colleagues,
bash buddies without consent?

Don't touch me. That always hurts.

Forgive the Monster?

In order to forgive his own son,
he would have to admit that his hate
sent the young man down that bloody path.

The son may have chosen to express
his despair by shooting those who lived
joyfully, as he was not allowed.

But, father created the conflict.
He taught his son to hate those who loved
as the son did, so to hate himself.

Perhaps DAESH inspired the son to
kill to resolve internal strife. But,
father convinced son to claim guilt.

Father probably taught son that his
god punished homosexuals ere
the son even learned what the word meant.

Before the son understood he was
attracted to other men, he knew
his father would despise him for it.

In a country so filled with hate, that
bleeds from gun proliferation, the
father created one more monster.

Getting Rid of the Gay

You can't legislate the gay away.
You can't murder the gay away.
You can't hate the gay away
or pray the gay away.

Among all peoples, even most beasts,
you find those who are lesbian,
gay, bisexual, and other.

We do not choose to love this way;
some say our orientation
is determined at birth or before.

You can't legislate the gay away.
You can't murder the gay away.
You can't hate the gay away
or pray the gay away.

No magnitude of vitriol,
contempt, threats, or violence can
force us to convert our nature.

We don't ask you to change who you
love, to give up your jobs, freedom,
homes, businesses, or lives for us.

We just want the right to earn
a living, go to school, purchase
a home, have fun with our friends.

You can't legislate the gay away.
You can't murder the gay away.
You can't hate the gay away
or pray the gay away.

We want the same things that you seek,
life, liberty, the pursuit of
happiness, and someone to love.

The difference? We don't require
you to forfeit your civil rights
in order to enjoy our own.

Words Matter

Epigraph:
  phobia (suffix) irrational fear
  misia (suffix) strong dislike

Words have power.
They use language
to justify
hostility.

Homophobic,
transphobic,
xenophobic.
Media terms

attempting to
explain why they
marginalize
groups of people.

But, they are not
afraid. They just hate.
I'll no longer
grant the suffix

to those who scorn,
despise, detest,
and disparage
Queers, Trans, others.

Use correct words.
Homomisiast
transmisiast
xenomisiast.

Force the world to
recognize their
motivation
for demeaning

entire lovely
populations
who look, love, live
differently.

Not because of
any fear or dread.
Just resentment,
loathing, disgust.

Let them bury
their rancor back
in the closet
where it belongs.

T

Yes, some can marry now
and reap the benefits
of tax deductions, joint
adoption, judicial
protections, medical
privileges, and support.

But marriage rights mean little
to those who can't walk down
the street without fear of
hostility, assault,
panic if they need to
pee when away from home;

When their boss can fire them
with impunity if
he discovers their birth
certificate gender
doesn't match the one
that defines who they are.

And the hate hurts more when
it comes from those who share
the acronym, who should
remember what it's like
to live in fear because
"normal" doesn't fit you.

But all too often, the
L and the G forget
about the T near the
end and are first in line
to hurl invectives and
demonstrate their contempt.

Gender Blending Fashion

Those who identify as #GenderQueer
do not let others define our wardrobes.

Men's sports shirt with cloisonné necklace and
matching earrings? Sounds sweetly alluring.

Men's button down shirt with pearls? Just perfect.
Let's add a pleated skirt and combat boots.

Butch haircut with glittery makeup and
dangly earrings? Just put on a binder.

Men's purple shorts with pink, strappy, sexy
sandals? Just what the evening calls for.

Formal gown, stage makeup, full beard? Add a
stunning voice and you've a grand prize winner.

Do I Pass?

Worried faces peer out from selfies,
beautiful people desperately
seeking acceptance from netizens.

Reporting on the changes in their
appearance and lives brought about by
hormone therapy and surgery.

Trying to learn which cosmetics, beard
length, haircut, or clothing guarantees
family's, friends', strangers' approval.

What voice pitch will keep them safe from the
trans misogynists who call them names,
threaten their lives, beat them in the streets?

Why in the world do we hold trans folk
to gender binary standards that
most cis women and men never meet?

Why are they forced to risk life and limb
just to use the restroom when at a
restaurant, school, even in the park?

How do we adjust the narrative
implying those who are Transgender
want only to pass as cis people?

Doesn't dumping strict definitions
of how genders should look, sound, and act,
grant every one of us more freedom?

Why must we accept the constructs that
society assigns our gender
or impose them on anyone else?

Instead of classes in gendered voice,
appearance, and gestures for trans folk,
what if we taught cis groups acceptance;

Helped them learn the difference between
gender identity and gender
expression; to see beauty within;

Showed them how much damage imposing
sexual- or gender-based decrees
causes just about everyone?

Braving a Hostile World

Your hands trembled as you handed me
the piece of paper, with a recent
date, explaining why your state ID
incorrectly said you were male. My
heart ached for you, in your late fifties,
finally able to come to terms
with who you are in the face of a
hostile world. How brave not to let that
condescending letter stop you from
enjoying an afternoon sailing,
despite security theater
forcing you to reveal personal
conflicts to a complete stranger. I
read the letter, even though I knew
what it said, to honor your struggle,
knowing how you must have debated
whether to forfeit your afternoon
adventure rather than share it. But
I shushed your whispered explanation,
assuring you I understood. I
took extra care with your paperwork
so there would be no chance you would have
to extricate that missive from your
pocketbook again. Handing it back,
I complimented your stylish suit,
acknowledging the effort you had
put into your appearance on this
special day, and wished you bon voyage.
I was grateful you lucked upon my
post, rather than the volunteer at
the next table with the two-inch cross
hanging from a chain around his neck,

and hoped the sailors would treat you as
kindly as they did any other
older ladies who came aboard. As
the world changed in the decade since, I
occasionally wonder how it
has treated you. Did your family
accept you or turn you away? Did
you keep the job that allowed you to
purchase an elegant new wardrobe?
Have you taken time, now and then, to
have fun, to indulge in a few hours
pleasant diversion, perhaps on a
ship sailing across Commencement Bay?

#BiVisibility

Everyone makes assumptions.
Assumptions make it easy
to pass for straight, to pretend.

When you only marry men,
when you never find the right
woman to share your life with...

When you only marry a
woman, when you never find
the right man to share life with...

No one welcomes those of us
who are bi. Not the straights or
the gays. We do not belong.

We must be confused, we must
be greedy, we must be sluts,
we can't possibly exist.

I've never hidden who/what
I am. But I also don't
proclaim orientation.

I advocate for QUILTBAG
rights without claiming my place
on the LGB spectrum.

So today, I leave you with
no doubts. I am and always
have been a bisexual.

#MeToo

One by one we raised our hands,
spreading the #MeToo hashtag
like wildfire burning the net.
Heart breaking, I watched women —
acquaintances, colleagues, friends,
and relatives — share their pain.

From attempted rape at age
nine to the man who touched me
without consent Friday, I
added my trauma to the
cacophony of voices
demanding that you hear us.

Youth through old age, women get
harassed, assaulted, and raped.
In this patriarchal world
men still believe they're always
entitled to our smiles, time,
conversation, bodies.

I questioned the tactic of
using #MeToo to drive home
exactly how prevalent
the sexual assault we
experience is. Perhaps
only those women who have

never been sexually
harassed or assaulted or
abused should be asked to raise
their virtual hands because
the silence might deafen those
who quickly claimed #NotAllMen.

If women you know did not
post their stories, it only
means they don't feel safe sharing,
not that they have never been
harassed, assaulted, abused.
Are you to blame for their fear?

Stop acting surprised when one
woman finally reports
a public figure raped her
and then dozens of other
victims confess that they too
were assaulted by this man.

Stop asking "why didn't she"?
and start asking "why did he"?
Instead of teaching girls how
to avoid getting raped, why
don't you teach boys not to rape,
to obtain active consent?

Women should be able to
walk down any street or ride
public transit dressed to please
themselves without fear that males
might use that as an excuse
to harass or assault them.

We should not have to endure
criticism for how we
look, whether or not we smile,
not wanting to converse with
any male who demands it
even if he disgusts us.

Girls should not be sent home from
school, deprived of classroom time,
because *they* are distracting.
Males (students *and* teachers) need
to learn that no type of dress
invites sexual notice.

Before posting #NotAllMen,
think. Have you ever asked a
woman to smile? Spoken in
a way that could be taken
as suggestive by someone
who did not flirt with you first?

Have you ever put your hand
anywhere on a woman
without first asking her if
touching was acceptable?
These are just a few common
examples, I could cite more.

You may claim your actions are
"innocent," but it's not your
interpretation that counts.
You don't live every day
in fear that the next man you
meet will be one who rapes you.

You don't cringe watching as yet
one more male celebrity
gets "another chance" — allowed
to regain his fortune, fame,
position of power, the
freedom to abuse again.

Women's Lot

At the beginning and end,
pro "life." Forced birth, forced breathing.

In between no limits to
anguish, deprivation, torment.

Starvation, imprisonment,
torture, medical neglect.

Dying to give birth to a
never-viable stillborn.

Incarcerated if you
take a pill to abort an

egg fertilized by rapists.
Or your father, your brother.

Arrested for uterus
rejecting deformed fetus.

Murdered by the state if you
claim autonomy over

your own body. Denied pre-
natal checkups, medical

care — during birth or after —
when carrying child to term.

No child care or family-wage
jobs. No food or medicine

for yourself or your children.
Suffering hunger, neglect.

Enduring poverty, poor
health, homelessness. Jailed for

vagrancy, mental illness,
defending yourself from rape.

When no longer fertile, you're
relegated to silent

obscurity, unseen and
unheard by society.

While dying, tubes forced into
your nose, your stomach, your veins

to keep you alive, in pain,
with no reason to live, while

you beg for release from the
agony, your bills added

to your descendant's debt so
their slavery continues.

Pro "life," not pro living; just
another way to oppress.

Who's Hurting?

You claim your life is decimated,
you're a broken man, suffering from
depression, anxiety, panic
bouts, post-traumatic stress disorder.

You lost the athletic scholarship,
the promise of Olympic glory,
that should be punishment enough for
twenty minutes of drunken action.

You destroyed your athletic career,
forfeited millions of dollars in
endorsements/sponsorships because no
one believed your intruder story.

You were just a teen, resurrecting
the attack decades later is a
calculated conspiracy that's
politically motivated.

You're an Eagle Scout, come from a good
family, attend an excellent
school. Someone should have told her just how
devastating a trial would be.

You denounce the alcohol, complain
about criminals, disparage the
party atmosphere, blame the victims,
deny the many accusations.

You ignore the dead, the traumatized.
No sorrow for those you've murdered, raped.
You only express remorse for the
damage to your own lives, jobs, futures.

You're broken, publicly shamed, distraught.
Yet you refuse to accept any
responsibility for your own
actions, whine about slaps on the wrist.

Your families bemoan decisions
that briefly shattered your lives and theirs,
tarnishing wonted entitlement,
depriving you of status, stature.

You ignore again the ones who have
truly suffered as well as *their* loved
ones who mourn, who support, who must pick
up the pieces and struggle forward.

You destroyed youth, ended lives, stole their
dignity, safety, pride; inflicted
pain and lifelong scars. Yet you will not
even concede your victims' torment.

She Only Screams at Night

When he returns home drunk,
when he trips over toys,
when his dinner is cold,
he beats her and she screams.

When arthritis swells joints
against nerves, when she can't
keep her balance and falls,
when gnarled flesh cramps, she screams.

When she's forgotten how
to speak, can no longer
remember the words to
explain her pain, she screams.

The walls are thin, but you
can hear no words, only
raised voices: male, female.
You can't tell *why* she screams.

You debate whether you
should call the police or
if it's better to just
respect her privacy.

Disappearing one night,
they depart only months
after moving in. You
try to forget her screams.

Still Fighting

The same folks who believe racism
only exists in the past will tell
you patriarchal misogyny
is obsolete and men now suffer
because women hold all of the cards.

They ignore rape culture, blame victims
for their assaults; refuse to believe
those abused by their spouses until
men murder their wives; invent numbers
to back up spurious assertions.

Women have no voice or power. We're
denied control over our bodies,
our employment, our health care, our
lives. When it comes down to he said/she
said, only the he's ever believed.

Even when there's multiple shes who
report similar incidents of
abuse/trauma, only the accused
must be protected while the many
victims are vilified, tormented.

Decrying false rape accusations
that don't happen, Men's Rights Activists
complain they can't get custody of
children viewed only as possessions;
begrudge women any small gains made.

They menace any who oppose them,
using patriarchy's power to
drive women offline and away from
their homes with threats of rape and death
while whining that no one will screw them.

Not Our Fault

We did nothing wrong.
They left 'cause feminists
influenced them against us.

We lost custody
just 'cause we never paid
support, took care of the kids.

Courts discriminate
against fathers, always
favor and reward mothers

Not 'cause we ever
abused or neglected
our spouses and our children

Only 'cause men don't
have rights anymore, we're
the victims. It's not our fault.

Explaining the Hashtags

#NotAllMen
Tell me how are you working
to dismantle the patriarchy?
You aren't? Then yes, all men.

#NotAllCops
Have you reported, investigated,
and testified against a criminal cop?
You haven't? Then yes, all cops.

#NotAllWhites
Exactly what are you doing to fight against
systemic racism and for reparations?
Posting on social media? Then yes, all whites.

#NotAllChristians
Do you stand up to those eviscerating LGBTQ
civil rights and reproductive health care access?
Didn't think so. Sorry yes, all Christians.

#AllLivesMatters
Have you done anything lately to protect
a person of color from racist cops?
Or did you call 911 on someone existing while Black?

#TargetLooting
The store specifically designed to
criminalize POC and the poor?
Do you find policies making it difficult to shop there acceptable?

#RiotingIsIndefensible
What if City Hall won't listen and peaceful
protest is met with militarized police?
"A riot is the language of the unheard." — Martin Luther King Jr.

\#PropertyOverPeople
When a legal system grants more value
to a white man's store than a Black man's life,
extrajudicial property destruction gives POC a voice.

\#PoliceBrutality
What if burning down a police station saved
a dozen POC lives, or even just one?
Police must be stripped of power and privilege, held accountable.

\#BlackLivesMatter.
\#TheyBuiltThisCountry.
They can \#BurnItDown

Point of View

You say revitalization.
But, I see gentrification.
You applaud expensive boutiques.
I mourn POC displacement.

You encourage "innovation,"
approve the gig economy.
I mourn jobs, wages, benefits
lost to tech bro prosperity.

Camps of homeless natives, displaced
by invasions of digital
disruptors, struggling to survive
working three minimum-wage jobs.

Scooters litter the street, short-term
rentals jack up rates, ride sharing
drivers assault their passengers,
"flexible" jobs don't pay enough.

Seniors, veterans, the under
employed have no place to live
while excessively rewarded
exploiters plot a move to Mars.

Intersectionality

When I study the spoked diagram,
even I am surprised to see how
many times I slip below the line
dividing those with privilege from
those without.

Seven rails have impaled me since my
childhood. One I only accepted
recently and still do not claim for
fear it will be labeled a cry for
attention.

Three I slipped down as my youth trickled
away; one I embraced freely to
pursue my muse. So I dangle from
ten of the fourteen palings without
privilege.

Those who balance on poles above the
line — straight, white, cis males most of all — can't
comprehend how their privileges
destroy barriers; pave over their
road through life.

For even if one or two shafts should
elude them, they do not encounter
the same barricades blocking their life
journey that those of us hanging on
below do.

I have a new test for privilege.
If you were at all surprised by the
'16 election results, I know
you sit above the line between haves
and have nots.

Only those privileged enough to ignore racism, misogyny, heterosexism, religious bigotry, did not expect fascist victory.

On the Fringes

I do not pretend to be white,
and there are those who would quickly
disabuse me of such a pretense.

I do not pretend to be Black,
my ancestral skin long ago
lightened to more acceptable hues.

But, my world view was formed by the
neighborhood children throwing rocks
at my grandfather, by their white

parents boycotting all of us
for welcoming dark-skinned guests, by
the Black girls who beat me up at
camp because of my heritage.

My life's journey takes me from
one state to another, never
staying long enough to plant roots.

While I may sometimes find myself
welcome for a bit among an
organization or small group,

at best I fit in awkwardly.
I've never belonged anywhere,
and I probably never will.

Growing up Jewish in the American South

Pogroms and persecution are my heritage.
Violence and prejudice colored my childhood.
Forced, despite my protest, to say Christian prayers
by people who refused to admit that Jesus
was a Jewish rabbi, just like my grandfather
at whom they threw stones and whose thick accent they mocked.

Both my name and my nose made assimilation
impossible in a culture unwilling to
accept anyone with a drop of blood that they
believed less than pure white. They created, where none
exist, artificial distinctions based on
skin color, rather than accept commonalities.

Watching the prejudice and discrimination
meted out by those I considered my friends, once
boycotted by an entire neighborhood because
of whom we welcomed into our home, assaulted
and beaten for a creed I never practiced, I
grew up angry about injustice, bigotry.

As my lifetime stretches past the half century
mark, I watch with dismay as the incremental
improvements of my early decades wash away
in the acrimony and hostility that
seem intrinsic to this time, much emanating
from the South I remember. I dread the future.

Chains of Injustice

Chains of oppression run through my veins:
my ancestors, my grandparents, my
parents, me — all victims of bias,
pogroms, hate, bigotry, prejudice.

That dreadful inheritance made me
sympathetic to the suffering
of other Americans — People
of the First Nations, those descended
from Africans kidnapped and brought here
as slaves, other folk with dark skin who
speak unfamiliar languages,
those targeted because their gender
and orientation aren't "normal."

I walk among those who refuse to
subscribe to the polytheistic
worship of vengeful father, kind son,
holy ghost, and almighty dollar.

But even for those who're excluded,
tribalism rules. Blacks beat me for
being Jewish, Queers ostracize me
because I am a bisexual.
Jews massacre Palestinians,
forgetting the Holocaust's lessons.
Buddhists in Burma slaughter stateless
Rohingya. Sunni and Shia brawl.

Although combined we outnumber our
oppressors, as long as we allow
them to divide and conquer we will
never succeed in breaking our chains.

#NeverAgainIsNow
(a Rictameter)

No. Pro-
Palestine is
not anti-Semitic.
It's anti-apartheid, anti-
ethnic cleansing, anti-genocide, and
anti-colonialism.
Being Jewish doesn't
require being
evil.

Protecting Hate
(by forbidding words)

Extremists employ
elite *entitlement*
to destroy *diversity*,
vilify the *vulnerable*,
torment *transgender* tribes, and favor
fetus function above aiding adults
and adolescents, while eviscerating
evidence-based exhortations and sabotaging
science-based strategies to delay our destruction.

Persecution

Five thousand seven hundred years
of genocide, holocaust, and
annihilation. Of exile,
wandering, and ruin.

My grandmother went to bed each
night not knowing if the Cossacks
would drag her out of it before
the morning sun rose.

My mother's parents ran from the
revolution. They'd thought with the
Czar dead oppression would end, but
pogroms continued.

My grandfather's family was
forced to leave their ancestral lands
while the British, Arabs, and Turks
bickered over it.

How many relatives I will
never know were massacred at
Treblinka, Auschwitz, Majdanek,
Belzec, Sobibor?

My people survived five thousand
years of oppression, injustice,
slaughter, displacement, and many
more atrocities.

Yet, aggrieved U.S. christians will
allege persecution if they're
not allowed to deprive others
of their civil rights.

They wail about the war on their
holiday, while expecting those
who observe any other faith
to celebrate it.

This country caters to those who
call themselves christian. But like two-
year-old brats, if they cannot have
their way they cry foul.

Armed

I despise the weight in my hand,
the thunder of the bullets as
they hurtle toward targets, the
stench of exploding gunpowder.

I loathe the recoil that jolts my
fragile hands each time I pull the
trigger, the bite of the metal
casings ricocheting off my flesh.

And yet I practice my grip, and
adjust my stance. I aim, I fire.
I train. I research. I study.
We live in such dangerous times.

Heartlands

Middle class bigots and racists in
the heartland blame economic loss
on the "other" rather than their own
refusal to educate themselves.

They believe white nationalism will
bring back jobs lost to automation,
ignoring twenty-first century
realities, wallowing in hate.

They ignore income disparity,
suffered by working class people of
color who don't earn enough for food,
while grumbling about their "old" car.

They refuse jobs in fields and orchards
but berate those who cross the border
to pull the weeds, pluck strawberries from
the vine, and cut asparagus spears.

Outrage over thrown glitter against
blood on the streets; accusations of
obstinance from builders of roadblocks;
persistent privilege hurts us all.

Summer's Heat

In the Pacific Northwest we've a
love-hate relationship with the sun.
While we treasure our short Summer for
blue skies and joyous celebrations,
the natives sigh with relief when Fall's
first rain brings water to thirsty plants.

Though winter skies are ever dreary,
Spring's vibrant colors compensate for
months of precipitation. Here we
know the difference between drizzles
and sprinkles, cloudbursts and showers;
applaud brief sun break appearances.

But now summers last too long. Spring rains
refuse to fall. Winter's snow pack shrinks
every year, cutting skiing time short.
Fire season starts earlier and lasts
longer, kills more firefighters, burns more
acres, and destroys more homes each year.

Perhaps we should beg Lono to cross
the ocean and join Pele whose fire
rumbles under our feet, threatening
to burst from the peaks surrounding us,
and tear asunder the land on which
we build houses and cultivate food.

Maybe if we welcome the old gods,
eschew worshiping the trinity
of money, power, and oil,
we can avoid inclusion among
the species eliminated in
the planet's sixth wave of extinction.

Forgotten

Fire sweeps across the west,
burning fields, forests,
houses, and boats.

Drought parches farmland from
Pacific coastal
states to Rockies.

Seas rise, encroaching on
beaches, putting the
islands at risk.

Storms tear through our cities
during fall, winter,
summer, and spring.

Yet still those in power
deny climate change
even exists.

At best they'll blame nature,
claim humans are not
responsible.

They refute the data,
ignore evidence
of their own eyes.

And so we've reached the point
of no return, when
we can't survive.

The planet will continue
happier without
such parasites.

All that we've taken, we've
built, we've learned, soon will
be forgotten.

Erased
(a Nonet)

Centuries, millennia, to build.
Yet all destroyed in an hour, a
day, a year or two at most
by fanaticism,
fossil fuels, plastic,
bigotry, guns,
ignorance,
wildfires,
hate.

Acknowledgments

The following poems previously appeared in these publications:

11/9: The Fall of American Democracy	"Growing up Jewish in the American South" "What Racism?"
As the World Burns: Writers and Artists Reflect on a World Gone Mad	"'Nice' People" "Thin Blue Lie" "Times that Try"
The BeZine	"The Hypocrite's Creed" "Normal Life" "Times that Try"
Black Lives Have Always Mattered	"Where Have You Been?"
CHAOS: The Poetry Vortex	"Normal Life"
Food ♦ Family ♦ Friends by F.I. Goldhaber	"Growing up Jewish in the American South" "On the Fringes" "Persecution"
Fredericksburg Literary and Art Review	"On the Fringes"
The Handy, Uncapped Pen	"The Cost of Staying Alive" "Privileged" "That Hurts"
Kosmos Journal We the World 11 Days of Unity campaign	"Chains of Injustice"
NATIONALISM: (Mis)Understanding Donald Trump's Capitalism, Racism, Global Politics, International Trade and Media Wars	"Amendment XIV" "The War on Terrorism"

The New Verse News	"Hate" "Home Grown Terrorism" "Little Old *White* Lady" "Respecting Beliefs" "Shared Grieving" "Summer's Heat" "Trans Pacific Partnership"
Outcast	"Do I Pass?"
Pink Panther Magazine	"Armed"
Placeholder Magazine	"Braving a Hostile World" "Hate Speech ≠ Free Speech" "Lessons from Martin Niemöller"
Poetic Medicine	"Not Enough"
Poetic Sun	"Grief"
POETiCA REViEW	"America the Beautiful" "Explaining the Hashtags"
Portland Metrozine	"#MeToo" "Forgotten" "Point of View" "Protest" "She Only Screams at Night" "Women's Lot" "Words Matter"
protestpoems.org	"March 10, 2011"
Rat's Ass Review	"Gender Blending Fashion"
Room's Turtle Island Responds	"Still Fighting"
Soul-Lit: a journal of spiritual poetry	"T"
Star 82 Review	"Armed"

Subversive Verse
  by F.I. Goldhaber

"Hate"
"T"
"Urban Warfare"

Take a Stand: Art Against Hate   "Take The Knee"

Tiny Tim Literary Review

"Begging for Help"
"Intersectionality"
"The Price of Prisons for Profit"

The Trick Is To Keep Breathing

"Blame Not the Virus"
"Disruptions"
"Eugenics"

Weatherbeaten

"#BiVisibility"
"Portland Heroes"
"True Colors and False Flags"

About the Author

F.I. Goldhaber's words capture people, places, and politics with a photographer's eye and a poet's soul. As a reporter, editor, business writer, and marketing communications consultant, they produced news stories, feature articles, editorial columns, and reviews for newspapers, corporations, governments, and non-profits in five states. Now paper, plastic, electronic, plastic, and audio magazines, books, newspapers, calendars, broadsides, and street signs display their poetry, fiction, and essays. More than 230 of their poems appear in almost 80 publications, including four other collections. In addition, F.I. shares their words throughout the Pacific Northwest and on the radio. They appeared at venues such as Wordstock, Oregon Literary Review, galleries, coffee houses, bars, bookstores, record shops, art events, libraries, and community colleges.

www.goldhaber.net